Animal Journeys

Edited By Briony Kearney

First published in Great Britain in 2023 by:

Young Writers
Remus House
Coltsfoot Drive
Peterborough
PE2 9BF
Telephone: 01733 890066
Website: www.youngwriters.co.uk

All Rights Reserved
Book Design by Ashley Janson
© Copyright Contributors 2023
Softback ISBN 978-1-80459-767-5

Printed and bound in the UK by BookPrintingUK
Website: www.bookprintinguk.com
YB0556Q

FOREWORD

Dear Reader,

Welcome to this book packed full of feathery, furry and scaly friends!

Young Writers' Poetry Safari competition was specifically designed for 4-7 year-olds as a fun introduction to poetry and as a way to think about the world of animals. They could write about pets, exotic animals, dinosaurs or even make up their own crazy creature! From this starting point, the poems could be as simple or as elaborate as the writer wanted, using imagination and descriptive language.

Given the young age of the entrants, we have tried to include as many poems as possible. Here at Young Writers we believe that seeing their work in print will inspire a love of reading and writing and give these young poets the confidence to develop their skills in the future. Poetry is a wonderful way to introduce young children to the idea of rhyme and rhythm and helps learning and development of communication, language and literacy skills.

These young poets have used their creative writing abilities, sentence structure skills, thoughtful vocabulary and most importantly, their imaginations, to make their poems and the animals within them come alive. I hope you enjoy reading them as much as we have.

CONTENTS

Aberdour School, Burgh Heath

Scarlett Nicolau (6)	1
Matilda Guise (6)	2
Laurence Paice (6)	4
Elise Sabol (6)	6
Laura Harris (6)	7
Felix Jakobsen (6)	8
Lily Sothinathan (6)	9
Kal Patel (6)	10
Leonie Staunton (6)	11
Alba Estevez (6)	12
Isla Doyle (6)	13
Benjamin Yu (6)	14
Max Cornelius (6)	15
Harry Mason (6)	16
Henry Cornet (5)	17
Oscar Coles (6)	18
Shivam Japal (6)	19
Thomas Shanks (6)	20
Alpha Barnett (5)	21
Emelia Miller (6)	22
Marcus Bouwer (6)	23
Aleks Atanasov (6)	24
Theo Slate (5)	25

Brenzett District CE Primary School, Brenzett

Oliver Morgan (7)	26
Mya Smith (7)	27
Marnie Matthews (6)	28
Henry Body (7)	29
Georgia Brooks (5)	30
Edey Rawbone (6)	31
Kit Williams (7)	32

Arlo Wills (5)	33
Grace Tollett (7)	34
Ruby Gilbert (7)	35

Echline Primary School, South Queensferry

Evan Blackley (7)	36
Fergus MacMillan (7)	37
Jessica Treger (8)	38
Summer Bishop (7)	39
Esme Gould (8)	40
Saule Petrauskaite (7)	41
Gracie Taylor (7)	42
Aaron Donaldson (6)	43
Flo Walker (7)	44
Callum Black (7)	45
Rose Fraser (7)	46
Callum Pascall (7)	47
Olivia Taylor (7)	48
Flora Goater (7)	49
Mason Brown (8)	50
Tyler Jenkin (7)	51
Hazel Healy (6)	52
Alethea Wynne (7)	53
Sam Job (7)	54
Gregor Macaulay (6)	55
Louie Wight (7)	56
Tom Harris (7)	57
Millie-Grace Smalley (6)	58
Leo Keir (6)	59
Macy Cowan (8)	60
Megan McNicoll (8)	61
Martha Mackenzie (7)	62
Jack Whittaker (8)	63
Ailsa Deans (7)	64

James MacDonald (7)	65
Maddie (8)	66
Mia Arthur (6)	67
Sarah Sepulveda (6)	68
Jacob Chong (7)	69
Amelie Baillie (7)	70
George Haddow (6)	71
Sean Robertson (7)	72
Joseph Walsh (6)	73
Alba Barnes-Gordon (7)	74
Orla Harrison (8)	75
Lily McBrierty (7)	76
Artemis Serifi Cassells (7)	77
Lucas Fairbairn (7)	78
Zoe Gowans (6)	79
Ruaraidh Edington (6)	80
Ruaridh McKenzie (8)	81
Lexi Dickson (6)	82
Amelia Black (6)	83
Jackson Davies (7)	84
Joshua Austin-Bergenroth (7)	85
Carter Cruickshank (6)	86
Finn Verhaeren (6)	87
Coen Goodfellow (6)	88
Elliott Colpi-Vance (6)	89
Veera Sharma (7)	90
Alex McBeth (7)	91
Xaiya Nicole Jammeh (7)	92
Celeste Cruickshank (8)	93

Hartburn Primary School, Stockton-On-Tees

Thomas Stockton (6)	94
Max Sudlow (6)	95
Ruby Savage (5)	96
Ava Rayne Stephenson (6)	97
Zainab Ahmed (6)	98
Layla Curran (5)	99
Phoebe Maffey (6)	100
Sebastian Knox (6)	101
Eddie Stephenson (6)	102
Nancy Clark (6)	103
Thomas Burrell (6)	104

Elizabeth Fitch (6)	105
Alice Devlin (6)	106
Blake Ward (5)	107

Haughton St Giles CE Primary Academy, Haughton

Elliott Mills (7)	108
George Haines (7)	109
Anise Read (6)	110
Aria-May Nickels (7)	111
Elsie Watts (6)	112
Indigo Pearl (6)	113
Daisy Weaver (5)	114
Ethan Gaut (7)	115

Highbury Primary School, Cosham

Verity Meredith (5)	116
Jacob Woodcock (5)	117
Reuben Gee (6)	118
Eden Cooper (6)	119
Alfie Cassey (6)	120
Jasmine White (5)	121
Rafferty Harris (6)	122
Olivia Jones (6)	123
Gabrielle Barrett (6)	124
Laura Harlow (6)	125
Maya Iftode (5)	126
Bethany Nolan (6)	127
Logan Spencer (6)	128
Clark Spencer (6)	129

Pencombe CE Primary School, Pencombe

Issy Cook (6)	130

St John's CE Primary School, Keele

Anashe Makore (6)	131
Erin Parker (6)	132
Adrian Montero-Thomsen (6)	133

Otis Hewlett (6)	134
Alice Bailey (6)	135
Tomos Hughes (6)	136
Katerina Zhabolenko (6)	137
Jonah Royes (7)	138
Emily Clarke (6)	139
Harper Tomkins (6)	140
Reuben Neild (5)	141
Jesse Li (6)	142
Jania Hanspal (7)	143
Gracie-May Garner (6)	144
Logan Barlow (5)	145
Baraka Iyadi (6)	146
Ruby Buyers (5)	147
Eeshan Bhat (7)	148
Richard Udeze Jr (6)	149
Hadi Asim (6)	150
Emilia Brayford (7)	151
Alexander Ferguson (7)	152
Milo Herbert (6)	153
Henry Evans (6)	154
Danny Jones (7)	155
Ella Kimberley (5)	156
Jake Bentley (6)	157
Rana Itani (7)	158
Isabelle Holding (7)	159
Parker Fox (6)	160
Zara Banks (7)	161
Oliver Webb (5)	162
Bertie Keeling (7)	163
Kazi Abdulkhaliq (5)	164

St Mary's Catholic Primary School, Newcastle-Under-Lyme

Perfect Raymond (8)	165
Bianca Rathnamalala (8)	166
Milly Womble (8)	167
Maria Marin (8)	168
Olivia-Grace Opatunde (8)	169
Daniel Wu (8)	170
Pippa Furnival (8)	171
Patrick Walker (7)	172
Toluwa Taiwo-Bello (8)	173

Hannah Sebastian (7)	174
Athen Eldho (7)	175
Jamie Hitchin (8)	176
Nikolas Gogas (8)	177
Scarlett Hudson (8)	178
Annabelle Berrisford (8)	179

Tabernacle School, Holland Park

Sissaye Csiszer Gabriel (4)	180

The Poems

My Sweet Little Cat

T he tabby cat is a curious cat
A round the house, she hides in nooks and crannies
B lack as the night sky, her fur is very sleek
B eautiful, nuzzling into my long silky hair
Y ou cannot resist her little face when she is perfectly purring

C uddly and always looking for a warm lap to snuggle on
A s speedy as a fast car, she leaps around the house
T ake care, she might pounce on your toes under the blanket.

Scarlett Nicolau (6)
Aberdour School, Burgh Heath

The Fierce Tiger

T igers like to gobble chunks of red meat
E nergetic tigers have shiny sharp sensitive sparkly teeth
R ampaging fast tiger racing in the beautiful shining sun
R olling, strong baby cub tigers are playing in the hot sun
I think tigers are my favourite carnivores
F ierce and ferocious, a tiger defeats a rabbit
I n the wild, tigers keep dead still and as quiet as a mouse then they pounce
C ourageous mum tigers are very protective of their cub babies

T errifying tigers, I wonder if they can defeat a lion
I want to be an explorer so I can see what tigers are doing
G rowling at a terrified giraffe
E ek! A growling, scary, fierce tiger
R *oar!*

Matilda Guise (6)
Aberdour School, Burgh Heath

Grumpy Camel

C lever camels can blend into the golden sand
L ight-footed camels can run fast in the hot blazing sun
E ventually, the camel will need a drink after three weeks
V ery clever camels can run further than a cheetah
E nergetic camels can walk very far through golden shiny sand
R oasting hot sun blazing down on the camel

C *lip-clop* go the camel's hooves when it is running across the sand
A fraid of nothing in the desert
M arvellous camels carry people on their backs
E ek! Be careful of the camel's big heavy metal hooves
L oudly munching on green yummy leaves.

Laurence Paice (6)
Aberdour School, Burgh Heath

The Speedy Cheetah

C reeping quietly through the green grass
H iding in the long grass ready to pounce on animals like rhinos
E nergetic cheetahs run like the wind
E legant cheetahs fiercely running through the grass with their black and golden spotted fur
T iptoeing through the grass and running as fast as it can
A fraid of nothing because it has sharp and shiny claws and teeth
H ungry and growling, ready to pounce on animals.

Elise Sabol (6)
Aberdour School, Burgh Heath

Scurrying Squirrels

S currying squirrels clamber up the tall oak trees
Q uietly creeping to find her nuts
U p to mischief, she steals the bird's food
I see her bound across the garden as jumpy as a kangaroo
R eady for the winter, she carefully hides her acorns
R eally fluffy and her tail is like candyfloss
E very twitch of her tail is a message to her friends
L eaping from tree top to tree top in the breeze.

Laura Harris (6)
Aberdour School, Burgh Heath

The Sneaky Lion

L ions love to sleep in the hot sun
A frica is a hot wild country where lions live
Z ebras have stripes and they are a lion's favourite food
Y ellow furry manes going around the lion's head

L ittle lost lion as lonely as can be
I wish I could meet a lion living in the wild
O nly brave lions will protect their cubs
N ever pet a lion unless you want to get eaten!

Felix Jakobsen (6)
Aberdour School, Burgh Heath

The Lazy Leopard

L eaping leopard twists and turns and pounces on their prey
E nergetic, vicious leopards are very powerful and strong
O h no! The leopard is going to eat us!
P lease don't eat us!
A mummy leopard keeps her cubs safe and sound
R oaring loudly to call his family to eat the juicy meat
D angerous and vicious, the leopards prowl in the African sun.

Lily Sothinathan (6)
Aberdour School, Burgh Heath

Greedy Gorillas

G reedy great, grey gorillas keep their food to themselves
O n his back, he has fur as black as the night sky
R umbling, stomping footsteps in the green, hot rainforest
I t is as strong as a whale
L azing in the green grass under the bright yellow sun
L aughing gorillas hit their chests
A great gorilla is the king of the jungle.

Kal Patel (6)
Aberdour School, Burgh Heath

Daring Dolphins

D ipping dolphins swim in the sea
O ver the waves, dolphins leap and splash
L ooking for juicy jellyfish for tea
P erfect pretty dolphins with skin as blue as the sky
H ear the dolphins click as they chatter to their friends
I n the sparkling sea, they float and dream
N ow watch the dolphins disappear under the water.

Leonie Staunton (6)
Aberdour School, Burgh Heath

Teddy, My Cavapoo

C avapoo is my best friend
A happy bark at the front door to say welcome home
V isits to the park to fetch and leap for sticks
A loyal friend and mischievous ball biter
P layful puppy and white curly fur
O ver the hurdles, flapping ears bouncing
O h no! My cheeky, fluffy as a teddy bear, Teddy, has fallen asleep.

Alba Estevez (6)
Aberdour School, Burgh Heath

Crazy Crocodile

C runching, crazy crocodile
R ushing with its thrashing crashing tail
O ften lurking under the water
C rocodile *snap! Snap! Snap!*
O n its back are green scales
D efinitely don't look in its mouth
I ts teeth are as sharp as a knife
L ook out, it might eat you
E ek! Here it comes!

Isla Doyle (6)
Aberdour School, Burgh Heath

Prowling Panther

P rowling through the jungle looking for his prey
A s black as a misty night
N o one knows when he is going to pounce
T rying to stay hidden he is cunning and smart
H e is soft and smooth to touch
E very animal tries to find him
R esting safely high in a tree ready to wake up when it's dark.

Benjamin Yu (6)
Aberdour School, Burgh Heath

Chasing Cheetah

C reeping through the quiet jungle
H e is ready to pounce and leap
E veryone is amazed by his fast and powerful speed
E ars are listening to all the sounds
T he camouflage helps him hide in the long, swishing grass
A yellow flash like lightning zooms off
H e is safe at home in his den.

Max Cornelius (6)
Aberdour School, Burgh Heath

Chasing Cheetahs

C hasing, cheeky cheetahs like to pounce
H e runs as fast as the wind
E very cheetah has a unique spotty pattern
E ek! Watch out for the sharp pointy claws
T he amazing cheetah hides in the long grass looking for its prey
A bove the ground, cheetahs sit in a tree
H erbivores. Watch out!

Harry Mason (6)
Aberdour School, Burgh Heath

Leaping Leopard

L eopard is very still and stands like a statue
E xcited, he pounces on his prey
O h no! The leopard is too strong
P roud and dangerous, he climbs up a tall tree
A beautiful smooth yellow spotty coat
R ipping vicious claws scratch the tree
D o not disturb the sleeping leopard.

Henry Cornet (5)
Aberdour School, Burgh Heath

Mischievous Monkeys

M ischievous mad monkeys swing through trees
O ff the trees, they like to run and play
N ow watch the monkey climb the tall green trees
K eep the bananas away from the cheeky monkey!
E nergetic monkeys are as lively as me
Y ou can see the monkeys in the tropical trees.

Oscar Coles (6)
Aberdour School, Burgh Heath

The Gliding Eagle

E agles swoop and glide like an aeroplane in the blue sky
A lert, he sits proudly on his brown branch looking for his prey
G raceful, his wings spread wide as he takes flight
L ong talons grabbing tightly onto a flapping fish
E agles are intelligent and amazing.

Shivam Japal (6)
Aberdour School, Burgh Heath

Tall Giraffe

G iraffes are as tall as a tower
I n Africa, they munch and crunch
R each up to the juicy green leaves
A lways walking on dusty dry grass
F our long legs, yellow and brown
F ast running. Watch out!
E lephants and zebras are their friends.

Thomas Shanks (6)
Aberdour School, Burgh Heath

The Laughing Tiger

T he stripy tiger was eating some juicy meat
I think tigers need stripes because then they can be safe
G rumpy tigers trying to catch prey
E ating some delicious meat as the sun sets in Africa
R oaring loudly to wake up the sleepy tigers to fight.

Alpha Barnett (5)
Aberdour School, Burgh Heath

Bounding Beagle

B *ark! Bark!* Barking loud
E ars flapping when she runs
A lways on the move looking for fun
G ive her a ball to play fetch
L oves to run, chase and jump
E veryone loves to stroke her fluffy fur.

Emelia Miller (6)
Aberdour School, Burgh Heath

Zig-Zag Zebra

Z ebras zig-zag through the long green grass
E very zebra has unique stripes
B eware of the fast, fierce, ferocious lion
R unning zebras are searching for grass
A mazing zebras are as fast as the wind.

Marcus Bouwer (6)
Aberdour School, Burgh Heath

Terrific Tigers

T igers are as stripy as my socks
I n the swaying grass, he runs fast
G rr! He growls at his prey
E very animal in the jungle is scared of the tiger
R oaring and purring like a big cat.

Aleks Atanasov (6)
Aberdour School, Burgh Heath

Rushing Rhino

R ushing, rampaging
H orn is shiny and sharp
I n hot Africa
N ever run with a rhino
O h no, it's is stomping on my head!

Theo Slate (5)
Aberdour School, Burgh Heath

Beaver

B is for big beaver
E ats loads as fast as an otter
A s violent as a lion
V ery aggressive to other animals
E very minute they are as silent as a jaguar
R un if you see one!

Oliver Morgan (7)
Brenzett District CE Primary School, Brenzett

Hamster

H amsters are as fluffy as a pillow
A s friendly as a fish
M unches on lettuce
S neaky as a fox
T hey are as cute as a cat
E ats sunflower seeds
R uns very fast.

Mya Smith (7)
Brenzett District CE Primary School, Brenzett

Hamster

H airy hamster
A s obedient as a dog
M assive like a giant
S currying
T errible hamster
E ats fruit and vegetables
R unning as fast as lightning.

Marnie Matthews (6)
Brenzett District CE Primary School, Brenzett

Jaguar

J aguars are very aggressive
A jaguar is a good hunter
G ood at fighting
U nderground they eat
A jaguar's sense of smell is very good
R un fast.

Henry Body (7)
Brenzett District CE Primary School, Brenzett

Snake

S nakes slither about
N ever touch it, it might bite
A lways looking for prey
K ing of the jungle
E very one of the snakes is dangerous.

Georgia Brooks (5)
Brenzett District CE Primary School, Brenzett

Lemur

L emurs like nuts
E at greens
M onkey around
U p in the trees is where they'll be
R eally cute lemurs have long tails like a mouse.

Edey Rawbone (6)
Brenzett District CE Primary School, Brenzett

Snake

S lithery creature that has a marble egg
N ight when the beast comes out
A lways hunting
K ing of the jungle
E ats mice.

Kit Williams (7)
Brenzett District CE Primary School, Brenzett

Lemur

L emurs have yellow beady eyes
E ats leaves
M any run as fast as a bike
U p climbing in the trees
R eally beady eyes.

Arlo Wills (5)
Brenzett District CE Primary School, Brenzett

Puppy

P ouncing and whining
U pon the bed
P laying and leaping
P uppies are cute and fluffy
Y oung ones are cuter.

Grace Tollett (7)
Brenzett District CE Primary School, Brenzett

Pig

P ink curly tail
I n squelchy mud rolling around
G runting loudly.

Ruby Gilbert (7)
Brenzett District CE Primary School, Brenzett

The Cheeky Animal

It is as fast as a cheetah that is angry
It swims like a mermaid dancing majestically
It is as grey as the concrete on the path
It is as strong as a nail
It is as long as a measuring tape
It is as scary as a dark cave
It is as good at hunting as a bear
It is as heavy as an anvil
Its tail is as big as a baby
Its tail is as pointy as a sharp rock
It is as wide as a turtle
Its teeth are as clean as a mammal
It is as sneaky as a ninja
What is it?

Answer: A hammerhead shark.

Evan Blackley (7)
Echline Primary School, South Queensferry

My Pet

She's as cute as a fluffy cat
She's as fluffy as a fast guinea pig
She's as smart as a P7
She's as wet as a shark
She's as fast as Sonic
She's as hungry as a cat
Her nose is as black as a gorilla
She is as peachy as my skin
She swims like a fish
She's as talented as my headteacher
Who is she?

Answer: My dog, Lola.

Fergus MacMillan (7)
Echline Primary School, South Queensferry

My Furry Friend

It is as fluffy as a squirrel's tail
Its eyes are as blue as the great sky
It is as white as a ball of snow
Its ears are as pointy as a jaggy nettle
It lives in a dark cold cave in the Arctic
It sometimes runs as fast as a cheetah
It is as cute as a baby puppy
It is as sweet as a newborn baby
What is it?

Answer: A baby Arctic fox.

Jessica Treger (8)
Echline Primary School, South Queensferry

My Fast Friend

It is as fast as a bullet train
It is as orange as a sunset
It is as yellow as the sun
It is as black as gas
It is as fluffy as a bunny rabbit
It lives in a faraway jungle
It eats red meat
It likes to chase its prey
Its prey are lions and tigers
What is it?

Answer: A cheetah.

Summer Bishop (7)
Echline Primary School, South Queensferry

My Big Pink Friend

It is as pink as a flamingo
It is as big as a greenhouse
Its eyes are as shiny as crystals
It lives in Fairy Land Cottage which is covered in sprinkles
It is as sweet as candy
It likes lettuce like a tortoise
Its horn is as swirly as a helter-skelter
What is it?

Answer: A unicorn.

Esme Gould (8)
Echline Primary School, South Queensferry

My Chubby Friend

It has a big belly that looks like jelly
It has black and white fluff that looks like a mystery box
It has teeth like a yellow banana
It has a tail that looks like fuzzy sand
It has claws like a shark's teeth
It has teeth like a spiky shell
What is it?

Answer: A rat.

Saule Petrauskaite (7)
Echline Primary School, South Queensferry

My Little Friend

It climbs the trees like a monkey
Its ears are as white as mountains of snow
It eats a plant that is hard and crunchy
Its home is as green as fresh grass
It is as red as blood
Its tail is as long as a stripy dust cleaner
What is it?

Answer: A red panda.

Gracie Taylor (7)
Echline Primary School, South Queensferry

Banana Stealer

It loves bananas more than I love Lindor chocolate
It's as tall as a strong old oak tree
It's as fierce as a ginormous great white shark
It climbs like a rock climber
It's as fluffy as my nan's ragdoll cat
What is it?

Answer: A gorilla.

Aaron Donaldson (6)
Echline Primary School, South Queensferry

The Fluffy Animal

It is as black and white as a panda
It loves to play on the cliffs like a baby
It eats herring for breakfast, lunch and dinner
It is as cheeky as a dog
Its beak and eyes are as orange as carrots
What is it?

Answer: That's right, it's a puffin.

Flo Walker (7)
Echline Primary School, South Queensferry

My Pet

He's the king of the couch
He's as cute as a bouncy bunny rabbit
He's as fluffy as a cloud in the sky
He's as sleepy as me after karate
He's as good as gold
He's as brown as chocolate
Who is he?

Answer: Toby, my dog.

Callum Black (7)
Echline Primary School, South Queensferry

What Is It?

It is as scary as a zombie with blood on its body
It has teeth that are yellow like a chick
It eats giant fish like a shark
It has a ginormous tail as big as a castle
It has one eye like a ghost with a bowtie
What is it?

Answer: A crocodile.

Rose Fraser (7)
Echline Primary School, South Queensferry

Scary Animal

It is as cool as a cucumber
It is as scary as a wolf spider
It is as cute as my auntie's spaniel
It is as crazy as a camel in the desert
It is as brown as a chocolate bar
It is as slow as a sleepy snail
What is it?

Answer: A bear.

Callum Pascall (7)
Echline Primary School, South Queensferry

One Of My Favourite Animals

Its tail is as small and fluffy as a pompom
It can be as white as snow or as brown as chocolate
It is as fluffy as a teddy
Its feet are as small as a baby doll's dummy
Its ears are as long as a baby snake
What is it?

Answer: A bunny.

Olivia Taylor (7)
Echline Primary School, South Queensferry

What Is It?

It is as white as a swan
It is as beautiful as snow
It has got a beautiful horn
It is as shiny as the moonlight
Its tail is as shiny as the stars
It is swishing through the coral reef like silk
What is it?

Answer: A narwhal.

Flora Goater (7)
Echline Primary School, South Queensferry

My Orange Friend

It is as orange as the sun
It is as furry as a lion
It is as cute as a baby
Its teeth are as sharp as glass
It is as cuddly as a teddy bear
It is as noisy as a car
It lives in a home
What is it?

Answer: My cat, Alfie.

Mason Brown (8)
Echline Primary School, South Queensferry

What Is It?

It is cheeky like a gibbon
It has a curly tail like a crazy pig
It is stripy like a wild zebra
It swings from tree to tree but not a hungry gorilla
Its colours are black and white like a fast cat
What is it?

Answer: A monkey.

Tyler Jenkin (7)
Echline Primary School, South Queensferry

Fastest Animal In The World

It is as fast as a racing motorbike
It is as spotty as a ladybug in my garden
It is as fierce as a hungry tiger
It is as hungry as a greedy goat
It roars in Africa
It is as loud as a lion
What is it?

Answer: A cheetah.

Hazel Healy (6)
Echline Primary School, South Queensferry

Lovely Fluffball

It is as fluffy as a newborn baby kitten
It is as kind as my uncle's Westley and Wayne
It is as bouncy as a baby kangaroo
It is as cute as a foal running in a field
It is as soft as a puppy
What is it?

Answer: A bunny.

Alethea Wynne (7)
Echline Primary School, South Queensferry

My Friend

She is as cute as a guinea pig
She jumps as high as a kangaroo
She is as soft as a lion's mane
She is as kind as me
She is as funny as a clown
She is as fluffy as a marshmallow
Who is she?

Answer: My cat, Lola.

Sam Job (7)
Echline Primary School, South Queensferry

What Is It?

Its eyes are as black as shadows
It is as bright as the stars
It is as sparkly as a shooting star
Its skin is as thick as a boulder
Its teeth are as sharp as a crocodile's teeth
What is it?

Answer: A rattlesnake.

Gregor Macaulay (6)
Echline Primary School, South Queensferry

The Cool Animal

It is as cute as a teddy bear
It is white and brown
It is not as cheeky as a puppy
It is as fluffy as cotton wool
It is as hungry as a greedy goat
It squeals like a squealing mouse
What is it?

Answer: A dog.

Louie Wight (7)
Echline Primary School, South Queensferry

The Cheeky Animal

It is as cheeky as a troublemaker
It is as cute as a tiny puppy
It is as fluffy as my favourite teddy bear
It is as fantastic as a hungry cheetah
It is as good as a sloth at climbing
What is it?

Answer: A monkey.

Tom Harris (7)
Echline Primary School, South Queensferry

The Cuddly Animal

He's as cuddly as a little bear
He's as fluffy as a pompom
He's as small as a tiny mouse
He sunbathes like my mum in Florida
He acts as if he is the king of my house
Who is he?

Answer: My dog, Alfie.

Millie-Grace Smalley (6)
Echline Primary School, South Queensferry

What Is It?

It is as powerful as a barn owl
It is as golden as the rock gold
It is as feathered as a black albatross
It is as large as a white buzzard
It is as fast as a spotty leopard
What is it?

Answer: A golden eagle.

Leo Keir (6)
Echline Primary School, South Queensferry

My Pet

It is as fluffy as a hamster
It is as sweet as a lollipop
It is as smelly as wet grass
It has four big legs
It is as cheeky as a monkey
It pants like a steamtrain
What is it?

Answer: My pet dog, Hunter.

Macy Cowan (8)
Echline Primary School, South Queensferry

My Little Friend

She is as fluffy as a puppy
She is as cute as a bunny
Her eyes are as green as emeralds
She is as silly as a kitten
She is as small as a hamster
She loves to play
Who is she?

Answer: Pie, the duckling.

Megan McNicoll (8)
Echline Primary School, South Queensferry

My Fuzzy Friend

It is as slow as a snail
It is as brown as a tree trunk
It is so lazy that it won't get up
It lives up in the trees like a monkey
It is as fuzzy as a Jack Russell
What is it?

Answer: A super slow sloth.

Martha Mackenzie (7)
Echline Primary School, South Queensferry

Slippery Scales

It is as slippery as the sea
It is as scaly as a snake
It has no legs unlike a table
It is as slow as a tortoise
It is as slimy as slime
It is as orange as an orange
What is it?

Answer: A goldfish.

Jack Whittaker (8)
Echline Primary School, South Queensferry

Cute, Fluffy And Chubby

It's as cute as a puppy
It can be brown, black and white or blonde
It is as harmless as snow
It is as small as a mouse
It lives in a cage that is like its happy home
What is it?

Answer: A hamster.

Ailsa Deans (7)
Echline Primary School, South Queensferry

What Is It?

It is as cute as a fluffy rabbit
It is as sleepy as an angry gorilla
It is as wet as lots of rain
It is as cheerful as a cheeky monkey
It is as happy as a happy emoji face
What is it?

Answer: A puppy.

James MacDonald (7)
Echline Primary School, South Queensferry

My Pet

He is as cuddly as a teddy bear
He is as tall as my mum
He is as playful as a monkey
He is as sneaky as a thief
He is as fluffy as snow
He is as cute as a bunny
Who is he?

Answer: My dog, Solo.

Maddie (8)
Echline Primary School, South Queensferry

What Is It?

It is cute like a spotty puppy
It is playful like a kind kid
It is as stripy as a black and white tiger
It is as soft as a brown teddy bear
It is as fluffy as a pillow
What is it?

Answer: A cat.

Mia Arthur (6)
Echline Primary School, South Queensferry

The Cute Animal

It is as fluffy as a soft pompom
It is as cheeky as a crazy monkey
it is as crazy as a camel in the desert
It is as sleepy as a slow sloth
It is as cute as a peach
What is it?

Answer: A puppy.

Sarah Sepulveda (6)
Echline Primary School, South Queensferry

Sealife

It is bigger than the biggest dinosaur
It camouflages in the sea
It comes up for air
It is longer than five elephants
It is as tall as two double-decker buses
What is it?

Answer: A blue whale.

Jacob Chong (7)
Echline Primary School, South Queensferry

My Beautiful Animal

It is as pink as a flamingo
It is as fluffy as lots of puppies
Its horn is as cool as an ice cube
It has four legs like tree trunks
It is as sweet as a lollipop
What is it?

Answer: A unicorn.

Amelie Baillie (7)
Echline Primary School, South Queensferry

What Is It?

It is as slow as an old man
Its claws are as sharp as spikes
Its scales are as rough as a brick
Its tail is as tiny as a worm
Its back is as thick as cardboard
What is it?

Answer: A tortoise.

George Haddow (6)
Echline Primary School, South Queensferry

My Tiny Friend

It loves to eat nuts
It is as red as a fox
Its tail is as fluffy as a dog
It is as fast as a leopard
It lives in the woodlands
It climbs up high trees
What is it?

Answer: A squirrel.

Sean Robertson (7)
Echline Primary School, South Queensferry

My Animal, Jasper

It is as cute as a cat
It is as fast as a spotty cheetah
It is as scary as a trapdoor spider
It is as fluffy as a bunny rabbit
It is as cuddly as my mum
Who is it?

Answer: My dog, Jasper.

Joseph Walsh (6)
Echline Primary School, South Queensferry

The Spiky Animal

It is as small as a hamster
It is as fast as a human runner
It is as cute as a baby monkey
It is as still as a crocodile
It is as spiky as a hedgehog
What is it?

Answer: A bearded dragon.

Alba Barnes-Gordon (7)
Echline Primary School, South Queensferry

My Snowy Friend

It is as black as the pupil of your eye
It is as cold as ice
It lives in an igloo
It speeds down the mountains like a cheetah
Its walk is like a waddle
What is it?

Answer: A penguin.

Orla Harrison (8)
Echline Primary School, South Queensferry

My Pet

It is as cuddly as a teddy bear
It is as sweet as a peach
It is as soft as a fluffy bunny rabbit
It likes its ball
It is as cosy as a hot fire
What is it?

Answer: Brodie, my dog.

Lily McBrierty (7)
Echline Primary School, South Queensferry

The Amphibian

It is as small as a germ
It is as fast as a cheetah
Its feet are as small as a bug
It has a tail as long as a rope
It climbs up walls like a spider
What is it?

Answer: A lizard.

Artemis Serifi Cassells (7)
Echline Primary School, South Queensferry

What Is It?

It is as furry as a bunny
It is as small as a rat
It is as cute as a funny dog
It is as slow as a happy tortoise
It is as powerful as a bad rhino
What is it?

Answer: A penguin.

Lucas Fairbairn (7)
Echline Primary School, South Queensferry

The Problem Animal

It is as scary as a skeleton
It is as fierce as a shark
It is as white as a snowflake
It is as fluffy as a puppy
It is as cold as an ice cube
What is it?

Answer: A polar bear.

Zoe Gowans (6)
Echline Primary School, South Queensferry

What Is It?

It is as cute as a bunny
Its tail is as curly as a caterpillar
It is as fluffy as a cloud
It is as smiley as me
Its favourite food is scrambled egg
What is it?

Answer: My dog.

Ruaraidh Edington (6)
Echline Primary School, South Queensferry

Browny Brown

It is fluffier than a dog
It is as quick as a cheetah
it is as sweet as a pineapple
It is as cheeky as a monkey
It lives in someone's house
What is it?

Answer: A hamster.

Ruaridh McKenzie (8)
Echline Primary School, South Queensferry

What Is It?

It is as happy as a dog
It likes to play in the hay
It is as soft as a blossom
It is as grey as a gorilla
Its tail is as fuzzy as a cheeky monkey
What is it?

Answer: A bunny.

Lexi Dickson (6)
Echline Primary School, South Queensferry

The Flying Animal

It is as small as an ant
It is as cute as a kitten
It is as spotty as a Dalmatian
It can fly as high as a butterfly
It is as red as an apple
What is she?

Answer: A ladybird.

Amelia Black (6)
Echline Primary School, South Queensferry

My Small Friend

Its legs are as small as seeds
It is as grey as a storm
It is as fast as a whale
It is as small as a mouse
Its jumping is as bad as a tortoise
What is it?

Answer: A hamster.

Jackson Davies (7)
Echline Primary School, South Queensferry

My Fluffy Friend

It is as fluffy as a cat
It has a stripe blacker than night
It is as small as a rat
It is cuter than a puppy
It is as light as the sun
What is it?

Answer: My hamster.

Joshua Austin-Bergenroth (7)
Echline Primary School, South Queensferry

What Is It?

It is as cute as a dog
It is as playful as a puppy
It is as soft as a bunny
It is as fast as a cheetah
It has a tail as long as a snake
What is it?

Answer: A cat.

Carter Cruickshank (6)
Echline Primary School, South Queensferry

What Is It?

It is as brown as a bear
It is as fast as a tiger
It is as spiky as a needle
It is as small as a turtle
It is as smart as a dad
What is it?

Answer: A hedgehog.

Finn Verhaeren (6)
Echline Primary School, South Queensferry

What Is It?

It is as cute as a dog
It is as fast as a raptor
It is as furry as a teddy bear
It is as ferocious as a T-rex
It is as red as fire
What is it?

Answer: A cat.

Coen Goodfellow (6)
Echline Primary School, South Queensferry

The Colourful Animal

It is as black as midnight
It is as colourful as a bright orange puffin
It is as cute as a baby bunny
It flies like an aeroplane
What is it?

Answer: A toucan.

Elliott Colpi-Vance (6)
Echline Primary School, South Queensferry

What Is It?

It is as cute as a cheerful puppy
It is as white as soft snow
It is as soft as a fluffy pillow
It is as playful as a furry dog
What is it?

Answer: A kitten.

Veera Sharma (7)
Echline Primary School, South Queensferry

A Cheeky Animal

It is as smart as a smart P7
It is as cool as a long carrot
It is as fluffy as a fluffy cat
It is as cheeky as a gorilla
What is it?

Answer: A monkey.

Alex McBeth (7)
Echline Primary School, South Queensferry

What Is It?

It is as scary as a dinosaur
It has sharp teeth like glass
It is as soft as a bunny
It has a tail as fluffy as a jumper
What is it?

Answer: A wolf.

Xaiya Nicole Jammeh (7)
Echline Primary School, South Queensferry

My Fluffy Friend

It is as cute as a puppy
It is as fluffy as a toy
It is as cuddly as a pillow
It is as sleepy as a sloth
What is it?

Answer: A koala.

Celeste Cruickshank (8)
Echline Primary School, South Queensferry

Sausage Dogs

S ausage dogs like walking every day,
A cool animal that is adorable,
U nder his blanket, he likes to sleep,
S ausage dogs have a long body,
A nd cute little legs,
G reat little steps a sausage dog does,
E very day, it jumps on the sofa and wags its tail,

D ogs are special because they make people happy,
O nly dogs can bark,
G reat to play football with.

Thomas Stockton (6)
Hartburn Primary School, Stockton-On-Tees

My Favourite Animal

G orillas are black like a ball of black fluff,
O ut in the jungle, he hides,
R iding in the trees, so high up,
I n the trees, lots of gorillas,
L ying on the soft green grass,
L ike to be strong, tough, and rough,
A nimals are scared of him because he is strong.

Max Sudlow (6)
Hartburn Primary School, Stockton-On-Tees

Cute Dolphins

D olphins are my favourite animal,
O ver the waves, they dive,
L etting the seagulls fly,
P ulling the sky too high,
H iding the dolphins,
I love dolphins so much, I want one for a pet,
N othing is better than a dolphin because they are so cute.

Ruby Savage (5)
Hartburn Primary School, Stockton-On-Tees

Dolphins

D olphins are my favourite animal,
O ver the waves, they dive,
L eaping through the sea,
P orpoise is another name for them,
H appily playing beside the boats,
I love to watch them swim over the waves,
N othing is better than a dolphin.

Ava Rayne Stephenson (6)
Hartburn Primary School, Stockton-On-Tees

Turtle Facts

T urtles are as green as wet grass,
U nder the big blue sea, it lives,
R eally slowly, it creeps around,
T hey carry big shells on their backs,
L aying teeny tiny white eggs,
E ating yummy fruit and vegetables all day.

Zainab Ahmed (6)
Hartburn Primary School, Stockton-On-Tees

Cute Bunnies

B lack bunnies hopping through the grass,
U nder the ground, cute bunnies sleep in the night,
N ice, so cute the bunny is, they are so cute!
N ice to see them all cuddle up, so sweet,
Y ou are super super cute!

Layla Curran (5)
Hartburn Primary School, Stockton-On-Tees

My Horse

H orses are spotty, some aren't,
O ver the fence, it gallops,
R iding every day, horses are good, as they say,
S etting jumps out for Tiny and me to use,
E at grass, apples, and Polos, with sugar cubes.

Phoebe Maffey (6)
Hartburn Primary School, Stockton-On-Tees

Turtles

T ries to fly a lot,
U nder the sea, you will see a turtle,
R eally good at swimming,
T urtles, so shiny in the hot sun,
L ies on the sand with the rocks,
E ggs are laid in the deep sand.

Sebastian Knox (6)
Hartburn Primary School, Stockton-On-Tees

The Coolest Animal Ever

T he coolest animal that ever lived,
I live in the jungle, that is really dark,
G is for the grass it sleeps on,
E ats wild animals that it has pounced on and caught,
R oar is the noise it makes.

Eddie Stephenson (6)
Hartburn Primary School, Stockton-On-Tees

Cute Bunnies

B unnies are cute and very fluffy,
U nder the ground where they sleep, how sweet!
N ibbles grass, that's what they eat,
N ow they hop and leap about,
Y ou are cute, I just want a pet like you.

Nancy Clark (6)
Hartburn Primary School, Stockton-On-Tees

My Favourite Animal

R iding across the rising sun,
H iding its babies from other animals,
I n the desert, he charges angrily,
N obody would go near the rhino,
O nly rhinos have their one horn.

Thomas Burrell (6)
Hartburn Primary School, Stockton-On-Tees

The Hot Day And Cold Night

S low in the trees, fast in the water,
L eaves are my favourite food,
O n trees, hanging off the branches,
T eeth are hard and may be sharp,
H ot all day, cold all night.

Elizabeth Fitch (6)
Hartburn Primary School, Stockton-On-Tees

Emu

E yes so small, like little tiny eggs,
M y body is small and very feathery,
U nder the tree, I lie on the dry grass.

Alice Devlin (6)
Hartburn Primary School, Stockton-On-Tees

The Dog

D ogs are sometimes small,
O range dogs don't exist,
G round is where dogs go for a walk.

Blake Ward (5)
Hartburn Primary School, Stockton-On-Tees

My Friend Jay

I went on a safari on holiday,
And met a friendly giraffe called Jay.
Jay has a long neck and is very tall,
And he likes playing throw and catch with a ball.
He has speckled legs and knobbly knees,
And likes to munch on juicy green leaves.
Jay is yellow and has brown spots,
And is very good at tying knots.
He lives in Africa, in the Savannah,
And wears a cool, stripy, orange bandana.
I really like my giraffe friend Jay,
I'd like to have him round to play.

Elliott Mills (7)
Haughton St Giles CE Primary Academy, Haughton

Poppy The Wonder Dog!

Poppy is a mucky pup,
She always runs away.
When we chase her down,
She gets all muddy,
And it turns her brown as a clown.
When we take Poppy for a walk,
She finds a big stick,
She always rushes in the grass,
And hates when she is in the house.
She eats the cat food,
And she always sits on the sofa.
Poppy is super playful,
And she plays with the cats all day.
We all love Poppy with all our love,
Long live Poppy!

George Haines (7)
Haughton St Giles CE Primary Academy, Haughton

Cute Guinea Pigs

I have two guinea pigs,
Their names are Bubble and Squeak,
And they live in my house,
And they are very cute,
Bubble is multicoloured,
And Squeak is brown and her skin is brown,
They eat carrot and cucumber,
And Bubble's skin is pink,
And they play with each other,
They tag with each other,
And they have twitchy noses,
And when they are happy, they purr,
And they are very noisy.

Anise Read (6)
Haughton St Giles CE Primary Academy, Haughton

A Cheetah's Life

Cheetahs start out as cubs,
They like hunting and belly rubs,
Parents get all their food,
If they don't eat, they're in a mood,
When they get older, they can hunt
To find food in their environment,
Soon, they find a partner and have kids of their own,
That is a cheetah's life in whole.

Aria-May Nickels (7)
Haughton St Giles CE Primary Academy, Haughton

Lost

The monkey was on a walk and he had
Lost his mum and dad,
And he did not know what to do,
A cheetah came by and was a friend that the monkey knew,
The cheetah knew where to look for the monkey's mum and dad,
The monkey was glad
When the cheetah found his mum and dad.

Elsie Watts (6)
Haughton St Giles CE Primary Academy, Haughton

Poisonous Snakes

S lithers like you can't even see it,
N o one knows that it is there in the grass,
A ccidents happen because it bites you,
K nowledge if it is going to bite you, we will save your life by grabbing you,
E xtra careful if you see one.

Indigo Pearl (6)
Haughton St Giles CE Primary Academy, Haughton

Flamingos Can Fly

Flamingos can fly high, up to the sky,
They are very pink but they don't sink,
Flamingos can fly high, up to the sky,
They stand on one leg and only lay one egg,
Flamingos can fly high, up to the sky.

Daisy Weaver (5)
Haughton St Giles CE Primary Academy, Haughton

Slithery Snakes

It's green and slimy and stealthy too,
It lurks through the shadows,
Ready to strike,
It's never to be found beyond the ground,
It lives on the ground.

Ethan Gaut (7)
Haughton St Giles CE Primary Academy, Haughton

The Giraffe

The giraffe is very tall,
She doesn't like ants at all,
She has a dog named Jared,
She doesn't really like salad,
She really loves to go to school,
She thinks it is really cool,
She loves to learn maths and science on the hop,
But does not love the fizzy pop,
Her best friend is a banana-eating sloth
Who has a terrible and nasty cough,
Eating vegetables is her thing,
But the green vegetables make her sing,
Being a giraffe is lots of fun,
Let's go out and tell everyone!

Verity Meredith (5)
Highbury Primary School, Cosham

Bees

B eehives are houses for bees,
E lephants are big, bees are small,
E veryone knows bees are important,

M aking yummy honey,
A bee is yellow and black,
N ot scary like people think,

H elping bees make honey,
O nly sting you if they get scared,
N ectar from pollen,
E very bee flies high,
Y ou know it's coming when you hear it buzz.

Jacob Woodcock (5)
Highbury Primary School, Cosham

The Elephant That Could Never Be Found Out

The elephant hid behind a big tree,
He shouted to his friends, "Come find me!"
His friends went looking far and wide,
Wondering, *where did our friend the elephant hide?*
Maybe if we listen, we can hear him stomping,
Wait, is that the tree he's chomping?
The friends went to check behind the big tree,
"We found you at last! Yippee! Yippee!"

Reuben Gee (6)
Highbury Primary School, Cosham

The Lion

Oh, great lion king,
He looks after every animal,
No matter how big or small,
He sleeps on a shiny rock,
But when he wakes,
He is hungry for steak,
Lion is so brave,
He would even walk into a scary cave,
If you are in a cave,
Please don't worry,
Because this lion is cute,
Purple and fluffy!

Eden Cooper (6)
Highbury Primary School, Cosham

I Am A Gorilla

I'm a gorilla, as big as can be,
I'm fluffy and loving,
But everyone thinks I'm scary,
I'm very clever and underestimated,
But to help me, I would need to be sedated,
I'm critically endangered,
With few and far between,
Poachers come into our forests,
And are often really mean.

Alfie Cassey (6)
Highbury Primary School, Cosham

Cheeky Cheetahs

C heeky cheetahs love to hide,
H unting for food,
E ven giving their baby a ride,
E very day, they run really fast,
T ravelling a long way,
A nd everyone moves as they run past,
H aving a race with other cheetahs,
S leeping now, it's time for bed.

Jasmine White (5)
Highbury Primary School, Cosham

The Gorilla Escape

Once, there was a gorilla that was alone,
But he had a plan to escape his cage,
He used his might to break the bars,
And went on a rampage,
He knew he needed to get home,
He ran until he found the jungle,
With his gorilla friends,
He was finally happy,
Climbing the trees to eat his bananas.

Rafferty Harris (6)
Highbury Primary School, Cosham

Rainbow

There once was a butterfly called Rainbow,
Who likes to play with a train and bow.

From Monday to Friday she went to school
But on the weekend she had lots of fun days,
She loves Sundays the best.

The end.

Olivia Jones (6)
Highbury Primary School, Cosham

Gabby And Bunny

Bunny is my best friend,
She stops my tears,
With her bunny floppy ears,

She lives in my bed,
But thinks it's funny,
To play when it's sunny,

My furry, fluffy friend,
Together forever.

Gabrielle Barrett (6)
Highbury Primary School, Cosham

Giraffes

G iant neck,
I love giraffes,
R ipping leaves,
A black tongue,
F our feet,
F ur with spots,
E ating all day.

Laura Harlow (6)
Highbury Primary School, Cosham

My Dog, Lee

My dog is big,
My dog is brown,
Lee is big and lovely,
Even sometimes eating our shoes,
I still love my dog,
And he is my best friend forever.

Maya Iftode (5)
Highbury Primary School, Cosham

The Scary Lion

I am the King of the Land,
I have sharp teeth and claws,
I like to run and chase my tea,
Then I clean my paws.

Bethany Nolan (6)
Highbury Primary School, Cosham

Spiders

A spider does whatever he wants,
He likes climbing houses.

Logan Spencer (6)
Highbury Primary School, Cosham

Smelly Gorillas

Smelly gorillas
Smell like my daddy,
Like banana.

Clark Spencer (6)
Highbury Primary School, Cosham

Seymour Not Eeyore

Seymour is my horse,
I look after him, of course,
He has big ears,
Like a donkey with great fears,
I feed him every day,
With nuts, mints, and hay,
He sleeps in his stable,
Dinners on the floor, not a table,
He is always stood
In the sloppy mud,
I love Seymour,
And would not want any more.

Issy Cook (6)
Pencombe CE Primary School, Pencombe

Animal Poetry

It waddles to the sea,
And they live in Antarctica,
They don't like warm places,
And they lay eggs,
They love ice,
And some are fat or thin,
They are black and white,
They have a yellow beak,
And some are really small or big,
They eat fish,
And they live where people do not live,
They will never ever go to warm places,
And where they live is so so cold,
It is a... penguin!

Anashe Makore (6)
St John's CE Primary School, Keele

What Am I?

I look like a fish,
And I am a good swimmer,
I love to swim,
And I am cute,
I am black and white,
And I am a little bit furry,
I live in Antarctica where it is very, very cold,
I waddle into the very cold ocean,
I have a blazing orange beak,
I have little eggs,
I have little babies,
I am a penguin!

Erin Parker (6)
St John's CE Primary School, Keele

Animal Poem

It normally eats big eggs,
It can have different coloured scales,
It lives in warm countries,
Some are very poisonous,
It can be very long or very short,
It smells with its tongue,
It has the same number of bones as us,
It can see if animals are cold or not,
It's a... snake!

Adrian Montero-Thomsen (6)
St John's CE Primary School, Keele

Riddle Poem

It is black and white,
They lay lots of tiny eggs,
They waddle into the sea to catch fish,
They live in a freezing cold place,
They are really good swimmers,
They are cute,
They have a yellow beak,
They have wings but they can't fly,
It is a... penguin!

Otis Hewlett (6)
St John's CE Primary School, Keele

What Is It?

They have really orange beaks,
Some are very, very small,
Some are very, very big,
They are black and white,
They are very, very good swimmers,
They really like the cold water,
They have pointy black wings,
They could be fat or thin,
It's a... penguin!

Alice Bailey (6)
St John's CE Primary School, Keele

What Is It?

They are bright grey,
They eat small yellow peanuts,
They live in the deep dark jungle,
They have four strong legs,
They have short tails,
They have pointy tusks,
They have long trunks,
They have big ears,
It's an elephant!

Tomos Hughes (6)
St John's CE Primary School, Keele

What Is It?

They live in Antarctica,
They are cold,
They have eggs,
They are black and white,
They eat fish,
They live in the snow,
They have big wings,
They have babies,
They have one nose,
It's a penguin!

Katerina Zhabolenko (6)
St John's CE Primary School, Keele

The Jungle Runner

A kennings poem

Jungle climber,
Deer eater,
Goat dreamer,
Tree hunter,
Zebra scratcher,
Loud roarer,
Sharp looker,
Good swimmer,
Skin cutter,
Clever racer,
Tree scratcher,
Teeth polisher,
What am I?

Jonah Royes (7)
St John's CE Primary School, Keele

What Is It?

They have sharp claws,
They have long whiskers,
They are different colours,
They have different patterns,
They have four legs,
They are lovely,
They are different sizes,
They like fish,
It is... a cat!

Emily Clarke (6)
St John's CE Primary School, Keele

Riddle Poem

Some are long, some are short,
Some are poisonous, some are not,
Some live in the big sea, most live in the big jungle,
They shed skin,
They are really venomous,
They are all different colours,
It's a snake!

Harper Tomkins (6)
St John's CE Primary School, Keele

Animal Riddle

Some pounce all around the place,
They have manes,
They run so fast,
They like to roar so loud,
They are so fast,
They scratch you,
They sneak up on other animals
And eat them,
It is a lion!

Reuben Neild (5)
St John's CE Primary School, Keele

What Is It?

They are grey,
They have four big legs,
They are very big,
They eat peanuts,
They live in the jungle,
They have long noses,
They drink water,
They have short tails,
It's an elephant!

Jesse Li (6)
St John's CE Primary School, Keele

All About Amazing Animals

A kennings poem

Fast runner,
Sneaky cunner,
Meat eater,
Heart beater,
Terrifying pouncer,
Jumping bouncer,
Greedy muncher,
Food buncher,
Fearsome fighter,
Amazing sighter,
What am I?

Jania Hanspal (7)
St John's CE Primary School, Keele

What Are They?

They like playing in the garden,
And they have sharp teeth,
They love rats,
They like fish,
They like fetch,
They have lots of walks,
They have four legs,
They are dogs.

Gracie-May Garner (6)
St John's CE Primary School, Keele

What Is It?

They have two legs,
They have eggs,
They have black and white skin,
They have soft feathers,
They live in Antarctica,
They have a beak,
They waddle,
It is a penguin!

Logan Barlow (5)
St John's CE Primary School, Keele

What Is It?

They have very, very sharp teeth,
And are scary,
They eat small and big animals,
They have pointy ears,
They roar so loud!
Their mouths open wide,
It's a... lion.

Baraka Iyadi (6)
St John's CE Primary School, Keele

What Is It?

Amazing sharp teeth,
Small,
Colourful fur,
Love rats,
Some are vicious,
Cannot fly,
Can scratch,
Have a tail,
Likes to go outside,
It's a... cat!

Ruby Buyers (5)
St John's CE Primary School, Keele

Poetic Poets

A kennings poem

Loud barker,
Fast runner,
Fast eater,
Lazy sleeper,
Amazing protector,
Bone chewer,
Finger biter,
Lead walker,
Squirrel chaser,
What am I?

Eeshan Bhat (7)
St John's CE Primary School, Keele

What Is It?

They are green,
They have red tongues,
They are slithery,
They have blue eyes,
They have meat,
They are poisonous,
They can bite,
It's a snake!

Richard Udeze Jr (6)
St John's CE Primary School, Keele

Dog Poem

They have four paws,
They have a tail,
They have ears,
They have a body that you stroke,
They have four feet,
They eat dog food,
They have sharp teeth.

Hadi Asim (6)
St John's CE Primary School, Keele

What Am I?

A kennings poem

Fast runner,
Dangerous predator,
Animal eater,
Sharp grabber,
Lazy sleeper,
Pointy scratcher,
Clever sneaker,
Jungle prowler,
What am I?

Emilia Brayford (7)
St John's CE Primary School, Keele

Mighty Hunter

A kennings poem

What am I?
Fearsome fighter,
Deadly dweller,
Meat lover,
Deadly predator,
Humongous leaper,
Quick snuggler,
Hard biter,
Sneaky prowler.

Alexander Ferguson (7)
St John's CE Primary School, Keele

Riddle Poem

They are good flyers,
They are cute,
They are fluffy,
They have beautiful wings,
They have fluffy wings,
Some are pets,
It's an... owl!

Milo Herbert (6)
St John's CE Primary School, Keele

What Is It?

They have a wrinkly face,
They are silly creatures,
They have hurt people before,
They have short teeth,
And have black fur,
It is a chimpanzee!

Henry Evans (6)
St John's CE Primary School, Keele

What Am I?

A kennings poem

Big hopper,
Speedy runner,
Huge leaper,
Desert lover,
Speedy racer,
Baby carer,
Fun mother,
Jumping lover,
What am I?

Danny Jones (7)
St John's CE Primary School, Keele

Animal Poem

It is very fat,
It likes mud,
It has a big nose,
It has a big tummy,
They live on a farm,
It is very muddy,
It is a pig!

Ella Kimberley (5)
St John's CE Primary School, Keele

Animals

A kennings poem

Big splasher,
Ground walker,
Peanut eater,
Water squirter,
Big stomper,
Noisy splasher,
What am I?

Jake Bentley (6)
St John's CE Primary School, Keele

The Owl

A kennings poem

Wing flapper,
Night looker,
Lazy sleeper,
Noise creeper,
Morning sleeper,
Night waker,
What am I?

Rana Itani (7)
St John's CE Primary School, Keele

What Am I?

A kennings poem

Pointy scratcher,
Hopper chopper,
Fast runner,
Grey stinker,
Carrot cruncher,
Tunnel digger.

Isabelle Holding (7)
St John's CE Primary School, Keele

A Big Hog

I like to eat bugs,
I like to sleep,
I like to eat leaves,
I am a warthog.

Parker Fox (6)
St John's CE Primary School, Keele

Mystery Animal

A kennings poem

Night flyer,
High fighter,
Sight seeker,
Night sighter,
What am I?

Zara Banks (7)
St John's CE Primary School, Keele

What Is It?

They have four legs,
They are pink,
They eat lots,
It's a pig!

Oliver Webb (5)
St John's CE Primary School, Keele

What Am I?

A kennings poem

Worm grabber,
Fly grabber,
Pointy beaks,
Wing flapper.

Bertie Keeling (7)
St John's CE Primary School, Keele

What Are They?

They have tails,
They have four legs,
They have eggs.

Kazi Abdulkhaliq (5)
St John's CE Primary School, Keele

The Cute Cat

There once was a cute cat,
Who liked to play and work,
He was an animal
That didn't harm anything,
Except his prey,
His colour was red,
It had cute eyes,
And one more thing -
He worked for the queen,
He ate prey every single day,
And that's the end of my poem.

Perfect Raymond (8)
St Mary's Catholic Primary School, Newcastle-Under-Lyme

My Tiger Poem

Tigers smell like fresh, delicious meat,
Like they always choose to eat.
Tigers look like big, wild cats,
That hunt all night and day.
Tigers sound like a roar of victory.
Tigers feel all snuggly and soft,
Just like my bed at home.
Tigers taste like a fluffy piece of candyfloss.

Bianca Rathnamalala (8)
St Mary's Catholic Primary School, Newcastle-Under-Lyme

My Reggie Poem

Reggie is nice like lice,
He looks like a small wolf,
He eats carrots and he hates parrots,
He smells like Lynx on a sunny day,
With cheers that say hooray!
He sounds like celebratory singing,
He feels warm and he destroys the lawn,
That is my Reggie!

Milly Womble (8)
St Mary's Catholic Primary School, Newcastle-Under-Lyme

My Bun-Bun Poem

Bun-Bun is kind,
She eats a lot of carrots,
She's sweet,
And she is forgiving,
She is like a shining star,
She is relaxed, just like me in my snuggly bed,
She is sweet, cute, kind, and loving to everyone she sees,
That is my sweet Bun-Bun!

Maria Marin (8)
St Mary's Catholic Primary School, Newcastle-Under-Lyme

My King Lion Poem

Lions smell of meat,
All rotten like feet,
Lions look nice,
But they actually bite,
Lions make noises like roar, growl, snap!
Lions feel soft and warm,
Lions taste like a bad snowstorm.

Olivia-Grace Opatunde (8)
St Mary's Catholic Primary School, Newcastle-Under-Lyme

My Cat Poem

The cat smells fishy,
This is the cat's favourite dish,
It looks like a tiger,
All soft and fluffy,
The cat sounds like a baby,
Cats feel pretty,
They taste fish.

Daniel Wu (8)
St Mary's Catholic Primary School, Newcastle-Under-Lyme

Wardens

Wardens smell like fresh blood, real fresh,
Wardens have huge antennae to hear,
Wardens sound like shrieking sensors,
Wardens taste like rusty iron,
Wardens feel like brick.

Pippa Furnival (8)
St Mary's Catholic Primary School, Newcastle-Under-Lyme

Red Dragon

The red dragon can eat people,
And it can breathe fire out,
It can kill people,
And the dragon has good sight,
And a good smell,
And can hear everything.

Patrick Walker (7)
St Mary's Catholic Primary School, Newcastle-Under-Lyme

Giraffe Poem

There once was a giraffe
Called Riff-Raff,
He smelled like a cat,
He looked like a rat,
And tasted like a buffet,
And as sweet as a souffle.

Toluwa Taiwo-Bello (8)
St Mary's Catholic Primary School, Newcastle-Under-Lyme

My Katy Poem

Katy smells like sparkling fish,
Katy looks like a fluffy bunny,
She feels like soaking wet,
This is my adorable, cute, caring and kind Katy.

Hannah Sebastian (7)
St Mary's Catholic Primary School, Newcastle-Under-Lyme

The Duck

A lovely duck smells like a plant,
She looks like a snack,
She eats fish,
She likes to swim,
And she has got a sharp beak.

Athen Eldho (7)
St Mary's Catholic Primary School, Newcastle-Under-Lyme

A Cat

A cat hisses like mad,
It's a brown cat,
It's quick with reflexes,
Some people think it's mad.

Jamie Hitchin (8)
St Mary's Catholic Primary School, Newcastle-Under-Lyme

My Lion

Lisa the lion smells like rotten meat,
She is orange and white,
She is as loud as horns,
That is my lion.

Nikolas Gogas (8)
St Mary's Catholic Primary School, Newcastle-Under-Lyme

The Bon-Bon Poem

Bonnie feels fluffy,
She looks puffy,
She smells nice,
She doesn't eat mice,
She can hear lice.

Scarlett Hudson (8)
St Mary's Catholic Primary School, Newcastle-Under-Lyme

Bunny Poem

It looks fluffy,
It eats carrots,
It lives underground,
It hops,
What is it?
It is a bunny.

Annabelle Berrisford (8)
St Mary's Catholic Primary School, Newcastle-Under-Lyme

Curly Rainbow Spider

One day, there was a spider
Named Curly Rainbow,
He went to the funfair,
And a party,
At the funfair,
He went on a caterpillar ride,
And a long slide,
Next, he went to Mr Worm's party,
And there he ate cake and Smarties.

Sissaye Csiszer Gabriel (4)
Tabernacle School, Holland Park

YOUNG WRITERS INFORMATION

We hope you have enjoyed reading this book – and that you will continue to in the coming years.

If you're the parent or family member of an enthusiastic poet or story writer, do visit our website **www.youngwriters.co.uk/subscribe** and sign up to receive news, competitions, writing challenges and tips, activities and much, much more! There's lots to keep budding writers motivated!

If you would like to order further copies of this book, or any of our other titles, then please give us a call or order via your online account.

Young Writers
Remus House
Coltsfoot Drive
Peterborough
PE2 9BF
(01733) 890066
info@youngwriters.co.uk

Join in the conversation!
Tips, news, giveaways and much more!

YoungWritersUK YoungWritersCW youngwriterscw

SCAN ME TO WATCH THE POETRY SAFARI VIDEO!